DATE DUE

F.61

FAC - JUL 1 9 1983 CANCELLED		
APR 26 '83		
CANCELLED KEMPER		
AUG 28 84		
KEMPER		

Lost in the Freudian Forest
or
A Tragedy of Good Intentions

Other Titles of Interest

ASHEM, B. & POSER, E. G.
Adaptive Learning

FRANK, G.
Psychiatric Diagnosis: A Review of Research

FROMMER, E. A.
Voyage Through Childhood into the Adult World

GELFAND, D. L. & HARTMAN, D. P.
Child Behavior: Analysis and Therapy

LEFKOWITZ, M.
Growing Up To Be Violent

NIXON, M. & TAFT, R.
Psychology in Australia: Achievements and Prospects

SINGER, G. & WALLACE, M.
The Administrative Waltz (or Ten Commandments for the Administrator)

WAHL, R. G. *et al.*
Ecological Assessment of Child Problem Behavior: A Clinical Package for Home, School and Institutional Settings

The terms of our inspection copy service apply to all the above books. Full details of all books listed and specimen copies of journals listed will be gladly be sent upon request.

Lost in the Freudian Forest
or
A Tragedy of Good Intentions

by

G. SINGER and M. WALLACE

Illustrations by SCHOFIELD

PERGAMON PRESS AUSTRALIA

SYDNEY · OXFORD · NEW YORK
TORONTO · PARIS · FRANKFURT

Pergamon Press (Australia) Pty Limited, 19a Boundary Street,
  Rushcutters Bay, NSW 2011
Pergamon Press Ltd, Headington Hill Hall,
  Oxford OX3 OBW
Pergamon Press Inc, Maxwell House,
  Fairview Park, Elmsford, New York 10523
Pergamon of Canada Ltd, 75 The East Mall,
  Toronto, Ontario MBZ 2L9, Canada
Pergamon Press GmbH, 6242 Kronberg/Taunus,
  Pferdstrasse 1, Frankfurt-am-Main, West Germany
Pergamon Press SARL, 24 rue des Ecoles,
  75240 Paris, Cedex 05, France

© 1977 G. Singer and M. Wallace

Cover design by Schofield
Typeset in Hong Kong by Filmset Limited
Printed in Hong Kong by Wing King Tong Co Ltd

Singer, G.
  Lost in the Freudian forest.

ISBN 0 08 022242 0 Hardback
ISBN 0 08 022241 2 Paperback

1. Children—Care and hygiene—Anecdotes, facetiae,
satire, etc. I. Wallace, M., joint author.
II. Title.

649.10207

All rights reserved. No part of this publication may be reproduced, stored in a retrieval system or transmitted in any form or by any means: electronic, electrostatic, magnetic tape, mechanical, photo-copying, recording or otherwise, without permission in writing from Pergamon Press (Australia) Pty Limited

Contents

PREFACE

INTRODUCTION

CHAPTERS

1. Interview with Susan
   Extract from Marigold Golem's diary

2. Interview with Fred
   Extract from Marigold Golem's diary

3. Interview with Susan
   Extract from Marigold Golem's diary

4. Interview with Fred
   Extract from Marigold Golem's diary

5. Interview with Susan
   Letter from Trevor Golem to his brother Bert
   Extract from Marigold Golem's diary

6. Interview with Fred
   Letter from Bert Golem to his brother Trevor
   Extract from Marigold Golem's diary

7. Interview with Susan
   Extract from Marigold Golem's diary

8. Interview with Fred
   Extract from Marigold Golem's diary

9. Interview with Susan
   Extract from Marigold Golem's diary
   Letter from Trevor Golem to his brother Bert
   Telegram from Bert Golem to his brother Trevor

10. Interview with Fred and Susan

PSYCHIATRISTS' REPORT

Preface

At the beginning of this century Freud planted the first seeds of the idea of "child-centered" upbringing. Until then family life, including child rearing, had been highly structured so that every member of the family had their role clearly defined.

Some educators and mental health workers regard unstructured child-centered upbringing as the means of promoting a happier, less repressed personality. Other educators, mental health workers and most politicians regard this new child-rearing practice as the source of all evil and blame drop-outs, drug taking and violence in the streets on overpermissive unstructured upbringing.

This book is a fantasy of the outcome of permissive child-rearing practices. The story does not lead to either of the extremes mentioned earlier; that is, the nirvana of self-insight or the disaster of drop-out. The tale we tell may never happen anywhere or to anybody, but the story may be taken as a warning of the tragedy that may result from good intentions.

Introduction

Before we begin this sad narrative, we must first introduce ourselves.

We are two qualified, experienced psychiatrists, well-known in our own circles. The professional code of ethics prevents us from disclosing our names, but rest assured we are eminently respectable. While case histories of patients are not normally disclosed to the public, sometimes events occur of such importance that wider publication is of benefit to all. The disclosures we are about to make belong in this category. They relate to the tragic breakdown of a woman, trapped by her own obsession with a theory and the expectations derived from it that did not match reality.

We have known Marigold and Trevor Golem for a number of years, both professionally and as friends. Trevor has always had a steady career in the bank and was appointed manager of our local branch six years ago. His wife, Marigold, is a psychiatrist who, it appeared, was able to combine the role of wife, mother and professional with great success. They were an attractive couple who were the nucleus of an intelligent, liberal circle of friends. Their family consisted of a boy and girl, fraternal twins born two years after their marriage, and the pride and joy of all grandparents. As the children grew, they seemed the epitome of the happy family, to us and to everyone who knew them.

In her professional life, Marigold was of the psychoanalytic ilk. Before her marriage she developed a theory of child rearing derived from Freud and became firmly committed to the view that the rigorous application of this theory would produce enlightened men and women with superior insight who would be everything that her own generation was not. When the children were born she put her theory into practice and the nursery became a laboratory for her obsession.

Lost in the Freudian Forest

Marigold dishevelled and sitting cross-legged on the floor

Introduction

Years passed and when the twins were eighteen, just at the stage when Marigold and Trevor could relax their efforts as parents and enjoy the fruits of successful careers, this sunny picture fractured. Trevor came home from work one day to find Marigold dishevelled and sitting cross-legged on the floor, muttering to herself as she wrote in a little black book. She was surrounded by a mountain of shredded paper—all that remained of her cherished textbooks. Stunned by this, all Trevor could report later was that she showed him a diary with the same words written over and over: "don't trust Freud, don't trust Freud, don't trust Freud . . .". Unfortunately this extraordinary state of affairs was not transient and regrettably Marigold Golem had to be put into an institution where she is now in our care. Since we are such old and close friends of the family we have taken the case very much to heart and have spent considerable time trying to trace the origins and contributing causes of the tragedy. To this end we were compelled to interview the charming twins, Susan and Frederick, although we were reluctant to upset them further by dwelling on these distressing circumstances.

We must add here that we do not belong to the same psychiatric school as Marigold. We explained this to the twins prior to the interviews and told them that according to our method, they must try to relive the events of the past as vividly as they were able to do. They should project themselves into the past and act out their feelings and hostilities as they existed during these earlier periods, even if their emotions were now changed completely. This applied to their relationships to each other, to their parents or to any other significant figure in their stories. The story that follows is an account of our interviews with them, extracts from Marigold's diary, and some relevant documents that have come into our possession.

CHAPTER 1

Interview with Susan*

I think I understand what you want me to do. I'll start with the earliest part of my life that I can remember:
Because we were twins it was a case of double cot and double pram. I believe Fred and I were a pigeon pair of good textbook babies. I lived a life according to the pleasure principle and so did my brother. This mode of living means you get what you want when you want it, preferably without having to ask for it and certainly without having to pay for it in any way. According to Freud this is perfectly respectable behaviour up to the age of two and a half and since we were raised according to Freud and his disciples, we were allowed to indulge ourselves. But as a result of this life style, the constant togetherness in shared facilities often proved very constricting for us. In an attempt to improve the situation I used to push and pull, shove and tear at Fred's hair and clothes. Fred, of course, retaliated.
It was at this early age we learned an important axiom of basic economics: the law of supply and demand. No matter how considerate and loving our parents were, when demand was doubled, supply had to be halved. Not that we were short of material goodies (although we always wanted the same thing at the same time); but one mother can only give twenty hours of constant attention a day. So if one got one's full deserts, the other twin got nothing. Usually this fierce competition breeds hatred and leads to constant infighting. With Fred and me the hatred developed on schedule, but we soon realised the infighting was fruitless. The common weal was better served by presenting a united front, turning aggression outwards and woe betide our opposition!

*Since we tape-recorded these interviews, we are able to reproduce them verbatim.

Any character regardless of age or sex who was on our blacklist was given a hot reception, which consisted of screaming and throwing toys. If someone ventured too close, my special field of action was hair-pulling with a sharp twist to the left while Fred specialised in right twists.

On the occasions when Fred and I moved together we presented a formidable front. The type of visitor he disliked most was "the baby talker" who produced the most infantile gibberish with a grin on her face. When Fred got into the hair of one of those ladies it was a joy to hear the screeching. My own pet aversion was the cheek pincher with a nasal "goo goo". This type of behaviour seems to be most frequent amongst aged balding males and it is often very difficult to get a grip on their hair unless they wear a toupée. Getting one of those hairpieces is a real feat. You yank it off, slobber on it and throw it into the furthest corner. To see the red-faced owner scampering after it is better than an all-day sucker.

As I said, our earliest way of obtaining attention was to scream. As we grew a little older we found there was a less exhausting way of keeping Mother in constant attendance. One morning we were enduring our customary post-breakfast potty session, during which we entertained each other by various forms of showing off (at which we excelled). Fred managed to remove a boottee and attach it to one ear, which gave him a very rakish air. Not to be outdone, and with nothing else in reach, I grabbed my potty and clamped it on my head, adopting a boadicean pose. This broke up Fred. His hysterical giggles brought Mother racing to the scene. She wrenched the potty off my head, and to my surprise was greatly disturbed to find the potty empty. She called Father to the room, not to admire me in my helmet, but rather to stare at the empty potty. This unexpected concern was repeated by Mother whenever Fred or I became engrossed in our private games and forgot our "potty duty". It was clear to us that an empty potty was better value than a full one. This chance discovery was an easy way of getting Mother into a gratifying frenzy of concern whenever other ploys failed.

Other enjoyable tactics which our parents put up with included the porridge game. This involves spreading the maximum amount of porridge on all available surfaces, including the outside of one's

Interview with Susan*

Together we presented a formidable front

self, while never permitting a spoonful to enter the mouth. This particularly nauseated Father who would retire early from this game, but Mother was obsessed with the idea that some porridge should go inside. She would persist for hours and so would we. Although the game ensured plenty of attention, I was exasperated by my Mother's enduring patience. Despite the burdens of profession and family she never lost her temper. Even at that early age it became a challenge to me to make Mother lose her cool.

There was another piece of teamwork that kept our parents moving all the time. If a child in a cot keeps throwing toys out of the cot and a willing adult returns them, this can develop into a very lively game for both. Now, consider the case of two children in one cot, de-cotting everything they can lay their hands on as quickly as possible and one adult re-cotting all the objects in such a way that the two children do not run out of ammunition. It is only a matter of minutes before the average parent drops with exhaustion, although grandparents usually last much longer. But this is really kid's stuff, confined by cot or pram to a limited field of activity. Once you get out of this confined space, a whole new world unfolds with limitless possibilities of being the focus of parental attention. There are cupboards full of glassware and crockery which two pairs of hands can empty in a few short minutes. There are large unadorned walls, which a pencil, pen or paint brush can convert into colourful scenes. Again four hands are more efficient than two. Or one child may hide and the other one rushes into the house tearfully to report the loss of the beloved sibling. I could go on for hours about the things one can do to be the centre of attention.

Looking back, there seems nothing to tell you—it was all part of a very normal childhood.

EXTRACT FROM MARIGOLD GOLEM'S DIARY

February 2

Today the twins and I came home from hospital and from now on I intend to keep a scientific account of their growth and personal development, for my own interest and the benefit of science.

Interview with Susan*

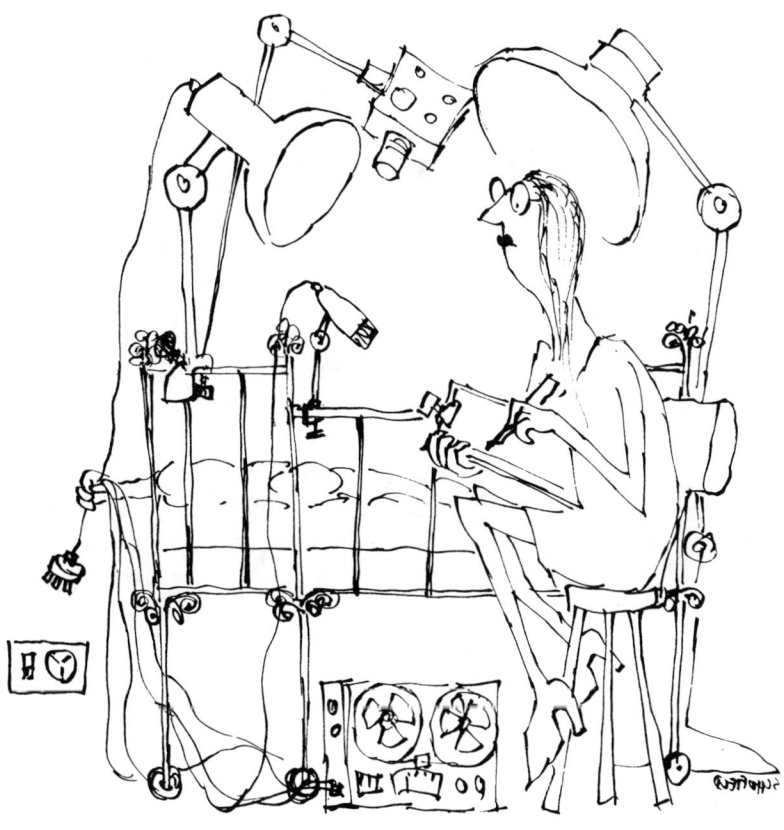

I intend to keep a scientific account of their growth and development

A patient who was mean, had a fetish about fur and was cruel to his wife

Interview with Susan*

My children are going to be raised according to the most advanced principles of child rearing. For years, in my practice, I have watched with pity as untrained parents struggled to raise children without the benefit of insights provided by such great thinkers as Freud, Adler and Spock.

My children will never lack affection, love or understanding. This assures a smooth transition through the oral, anal and phallic phases of their development which can otherwise be so dangerous for their psyches. If anything goes wrong at any of these important psychological turning points it can leave permanent scars, handicapping them for the rest of their lives. It was only a month ago that I had a patient who was mean, had a fetish about fur and was cruel to his wife. Obviously he had been frustrated at the anal-sadistic stage, a victim of faulty potty training.

September 14

It is most important that the twins should be able to resolve their sibling rivalry at an early age in order to be well prepared to deal with the two most important hurdles in front of them—the Oedipus and Electra conflict. For these reasons I was gratified when I came into the room yesterday and found them throwing toys out of the cot in a co-operative venture. I picked them up quickly and although it was exhausting to keep pace with them, I did so for an hour. I am full of gratitude that my insight into their development overcame my urge to stop them. They continued throwing, I continued retrieval. At the end of the day I was very tired, but went to bed a happy mother.

December 21

I was so excited at the twins' meal time today to find they both have a strong desire to cover themselves and their high chairs with porridge. Really, this absolutely thrilling display of externally directed oral expressive behaviour is most reassuring, and I consider it a triumph for my enlightened maternal care. Unfortunately, Trevor couldn't share this feeling of gratification. He left the table rather abruptly and I think he threw up.

The Oedipus and Electra conflict

Interview with Susan*

Thrilling display of externally directed oral expressive behaviour

March 30

Today was a cruel setback in my struggle to steer these children past the dangers of life. Despite every effort I have made I must face a horrible suspicion: *these children are becoming anal retentives!* Last week I found that Susan, after ten minutes, had failed to have a bowel movement and was, in a desperate plea for my help, drawing my attention to this by some rather peculiar behaviour with her potty. Trevor, who came into the room at the same time, had to retire doubled up with laughter, and he refuses to treat the situation with the seriousness it deserves. After all these years he still fails to recognise the call of the psyche. Instead he claims Susan is a show-off! However, for a week I have been worried sick about this failure, and fear my anxiety may have communicated itself to the children, because now neither of them will defecate on demand.

CHAPTER 2

Interview with Fred

It may surprise you to hear that as a child I often felt hostile towards Susan. It's quite different now, but let me tell you about me when I was little. First of all I was very good, and all my uncles and aunts loved me. When we stayed with Aunty Ethel I would always tell her when Susan did something naughty and she would give me a cookie every time. She said I was a fine little man and she was proud of me. In fact Aunty Ethel and Uncle James were always so nice to me, letting me have anything I wanted and playing with me all the time; I often wished I belonged to them. My own father never had time to play with me. He brought great piles of books home from the bank each night and paid more attention to them than to us. That's why I didn't tell him when one day he left a big black ledger behind when he went to work. I hid it and when no one was around, I stuffed it in the garden incinerator. Unfortunately, busybody Susan came snooping around and looked in the incinerator before it was properly burned. She knew exactly what it was and who had done it. I was terrified she would run straight inside and make up for all the times I had told on her. I fell on my knees and pleaded. I cried. I gave her my cowboy suit that she always wanted to wear. She didn't accept any of this. She dragged me into the bedroom, locked the door, and told me to stop snivelling and listen, and this is what she said:

"Now look here, brother. This is it. I'm tired of you pretending to be a model child, and buttering up Aunt Ethel, and always telling tales, and getting the biggest piece of cake and being allowed to stay up late, and never getting into trouble. If you don't want me to spill the beans to Father about the ledger, from now on you do what I say. Do you read me, brother?"

"Yes", I whimpered. Susan went on. She explained that there was

He brought great piles of books home and paid more attention to them than to us

a limited future for me in telling tales and currying favour at her expense, and that my come-uppance was not far off. She considered that as a lone wolf in this field I was devoid of talent. She pointed out the advantages of working as a team. Together we could conquer the world. I was sold! From then on we worked together. If she thought I wavered, she would hiss at me "remember the ledger" and I would shudder and obey. As infants we had worked as a team, and it had proved very successful. At the age of five we again combined forces and became a formidable pair.

EXTRACT FROM MARIGOLD GOLEM'S DIARY

June 3

I think I must have been mistaken last year when I wrote that sibling rivalry had been resolved. During the last few months there have been some battles royal between the twins. But after reading very carefully through some of Freud's case histories, I am not worried that the rivalry has continued during what he calls the latency period. Had the resolution occurred earlier, it may have been to the detriment of their normal development. There is so much controversy about the resolution of rivalry—it is almost like the dark ages of child rearing. Perhaps careful study of Susan and Fred during this time will allow me to make a contribution here.

At first Fred was dominating poor little Susan. He was a real male chauvinist pig. While I deplored this sexist behaviour, I did feel encouraged that he was identifying sufficiently with Trevor to want to imitate him. Trevor is a very strong man, which is the reason I married him. I need a strong man to prop up my independence, but our relationship should not be so transparent that the children copy us when they play "Mothers and Fathers". After all, we always put up a good front even when there is turmoil underneath our calm exterior. Anyhow, I saw Fred pulling the arms and legs off Susan's dolls and throwing them on the floor. I think it is an expression of his masculinity; he just cannot stand his sibling playing with dolls. He wants Susan to be a man like himself, that's why he bullies her all the time. On the other hand she is so female and submissive, running around pretending to be a fire engine just to please Fred. At Ethel's place she went even further in this endeavour and dressed up in his cowboy suit.

James thought that Fred was such an angel and Susan was really naughty. Of course they are pretty simple folk and misperceive most of the significant aspects of child behaviour. I don't think they ever have read Freud and I'm sure they think Adler is the neighbourhood plumber. Both the children felt a little bit anxious when they were away from home and overreacted. Susan by trying to become more like Fred, and Fred becoming overprotective of Susan.

August 26

Today Fred and Susan seem to have reached a turning point in their relationship. They were playing in the sandpit near the incinerator. I think they must have played "Family" at first. Fred was cleaning up after a make-believe meal and stuffing the remnants into the incinerator. Susan just watched and then she came over to him, they had a few words and he sank on his knees in front of her. (I wonder if they think they are still copying me and Trevor!) It was so touching the way they played together, a real Romeo and Juliet scene. All Fred's strutting male arrogance had disappeared. He seemed so attentive to Susan, almost submissive. However, I think it is very good for them that at the age of five, just at the beginning of the latency period, they have managed to achieve such a degree of mutual regard. Indeed a promising sign for the future of our society, if a man and woman can achieve such harmony so early in life. Sometimes, I believe that there has been an evolutionary improvement in the relationship which Alfred Adler depicted so vividly in his discussion of masculine power drive and penis envy.

What pleases me most is that Fred and Susan have found this harmony without my direction. I had the courage to wait patiently because I knew I had done the right thing by them in their early years —our Freud is so right. I wish Trevor could understand all this, it would make my task so much easier.

Interview with Fred 15

Masculine power drive and penis envy

Miss Crisp, the Director of the Kindergarten

CHAPTER 3

Interview with Susan

Kindergarten was a whole new world of people just waiting for us to come along and impress them with our charm and cleverness. First there was dear Miss Blossom in charge of first form, who smiled all the time, cooed when she spoke and was never cross, even with wet pants or temper tantrums. Then there was Miss Crisp, the Director of the Kindergarten, who had grey hair, big bosoms and a loud voice. She was a powerful lady very concerned that any decisions to be made, any actions to be taken, must be scrupulously "fair" to all concerned. An occasional member of the circle was Miss Rimsey-Smith who taught melodic sounds and rhythmical movements. She came every morning but made little impression (musical or otherwise) on our lives, being a lady of little clout. On the very fringe of the circle was an amorphous mass of mothers known as "Friends of St Crisp's Kindergarten". This auxiliary set up trestle tables in the playground once a week and a rostered band of aproned mothers sold fig jam, fudge and tea-towels to the unrostered mothers.

When we first arrived at "Kindy" we found a peaceful, contented, smooth-running community of little people. How dull! Even Fred agreed that something should be done to enliven the scene. One of the most objectionable aspects was Miss Crisp's insistence on fair shares, turn about, and the four freedoms. What a stifling climate for free enterprise.

A typical day in this child's garden of egalitarianism began with Assembly, which involved saluting the flag under Miss Crisp's martial eye to the strains of the national anthem, after which we marched off to Miss Blossom's nest. We spent the next half hour pretending to be trees and clouds and rivers and other unlikely inanimate objects under

Miss Blossom's smiling gaze, in tune to Miss Rimsey-Smith's musical accompaniment.

After play-lunch of milk and cookies we sat in a circle while Miss Blossom read a story. Everyone had a turn to occupy the most favoured position next to her. After that we were allowed to run outside and play with all the interesting things like swings, seesaws, tricycles and the sand pit. The tricycles were my top favourite. There were only two of them and naturally we were supposed to take turns. But how could I give up such a fascinating toy? Of course, I didn't. I just kept riding despite Miss Blossom's bleatings. The next thing I knew, Miss Crisp was descending upon me, bosom bobbing, voice loudly declaring that I wasn't being fair. The logic of this statement escaped me. However, force prevailed and I yielded the bike to little Stewart Throgton who always had the turn after me. The irony was that Stewart's legs were too short for the bike and he kept falling off. I knew he was really afraid of it, but the rule was that he had to have a turn. As soon as Miss Crisp vanished it was a matter of mutual benefit to trade my play-lunch cookie for his turn on the bike (a highly illegal transaction). This arrangement continued until I decided I wanted to expand my bike riding, but was handicapped by having already traded my only cookie. Somehow I had to make Stewart forego his cookie, so I could buy out fat little Belinda, who would always swop activity for an extra cookie. The best way to negotiate with Stewart seemed to be to promise not to beat him up. Next day I didn't even have to ask him, he turned pale at my approach and fled; the bike was mine without the payment of my cookie. It suddenly dawned on me that if he was in such fear of me I could probably have his cookie as well as his bike. However, I was puzzled, since I had never actually laid hands on him, as to why he was so afraid of me. I cornered him in the playground but before I could negotiate about cookies, he burst into tears and told me he would do anything I wanted if only I would stop giving him nightmares. The cookie deal was rapidly concluded. Although I was surprised to be credited with this supernatural power, I accepted it and the cookie gracefully and thereafter made good use of both.

As well as bike riding I became fond of the seesaw, the swing and the skipping rope. I easily monopolised these when it suited me by developing a variety of similar "persuasions", the essence always being a promise not to carry out a threat. These ranged from threatened warts and freckles to unkind names and violence. Each threat was carefully tailored to fit the individual. While nightmares were effective with Stewart, they didn't work with others. I had to find each individual's weakness. That wasn't really hard, people tend to play into your hands. In all of this I relied heavily on Fred to act as my *cappo regime* to perform the leg work, in return for a small but just share of the spoils. I soon became undisputed Queen of the Kindy.

You're going to ask me how I could get away with this in Miss Crisp's well-ordered world, and with our smiling Blossom as the constant guardian of first-form welfare. It was elementary really. The sweet and gentle Miss Blossom turned out to have an Achilles heel. Fred and I used to collect payola in a shady spot behind the infant's toilet block. From here we had a good view of the neighbour's garden and discovered that from time to time Miss Blossom slipped next door to flirt with the young Italian gardener and to smoke an illicit cigarette. Confronted with our accusing stares over the fence, she could hardly afford to report our activities to Miss Crisp. There was an immediate, tacit agreement between us which lasted throughout kindergarten. I guess I learned early that irresistible power consists of finding individual weaknesses and exploiting them fully.

EXTRACT FROM MARIGOLD GOLEM'S DIARY

September 8

Now that the children have started in kindergarten, it becomes more difficult to write an accurate account of their lives in this diary. I have felt somewhat anxious ever since I watched them going off with their little suitcases all alone into the big wide world. I suppose that *I* showed separation anxiety instead of Fred and Susan, but I managed to control it. I seem to be more worried about Susan in this regard. She is so small and fragile, she may have difficulty in coping. Here I am carrying on like an old-fashioned mother, it is really a disgrace. (I wonder whether I showed any of this at the last St Crisp's Auxiliary Meeting.) It was quite an honour for me to be rostered to sell fig jam at my first meeting; it is so important for the children to

Miss Blossom slipped nextdoor to flirt with the young Italian gardener

Interview with Susan

An honour for me to be rostered to sell fig jam

know that I participate in their life away from home. They must always feel that their mother (despite superior insight) is just like one of the other mothers.

September 11

When Fred and Susan came home from "Kindy" today I had a spare hour and we sat down together for a little chat. They told me all about the routine at St Crisp's, about the firm unwavering figure of Miss Crisp, a lady of strong principles. They were very impressed with her fairness to everybody. It encourages sharing amongst children, which is something I have instilled into Fred and Susan at a very early age. I think the combination of the firm Crisp and the patient Blossom will cater for the children's need for security. It provides an excellent opportunity to extend the establishment of basic trust from the home to the outside world. Such a peaceful, contented, smooth-running community of little people will ease the transition from operating according to the pleasure principle to operating according to the reality principle. The transition is a very important milestone in the development of the psyche to full maturity. This is one point where Freud and neo-Freudians almost agree. At least they do, according to my interpretations of their writings.

October 10

Knowing Susan's fondness for cookies, I asked her this morning whether she would like to take a packet along and share it with the other children. She said it really was not necessary, and that only yesterday she had given her play-lunch cookie to Belinda. I was very proud that she showed so much concern for another child. She is turning out to be a fine little woman. She was chatting along about all the other children and their little weaknesses for cookies or milk or a turn on the bicycle. She seems to know everybody's little foibles and is very tolerant of them. Susan shows so much concern for the individual. Her social conscience has developed very early and she is already showing signs of a precocious but liberal super ego. Liberality may be a new facet in the evolution of the super ego, a change from the

Interview with Susan

Transition from operating according to the pleasure principle to operating according to the reality principle

old harsh, severe super ego which seemed to emerge mostly during the Victorian age and in Imperial Vienna. One could speculate that this is the result of woman's emergence into the world of man and an increasing, genuine interest in community affairs. Susan seems to be a pioneer of this new breed.

November 2

Today I had a shock when Susan came home and told me about sweet Miss Blossom sneaking across to the neighbour's garden to have a smoke with the gardener. It seemed that Susan was upset to find her idol has clay feet. She has apparently internalised the mores of kindergarten society and seemed very concerned about whether it was fair to tell Miss Crisp. After reflection, I actually discouraged her from doing this and pointed out to her that we all have our weaknesses, even grown-ups. What worries me most, though, was that I felt a pang of jealousy at Susan regarding Miss Blossom as a substitute mother figure. I hope the adoption of a new mother does not require her to go through the resolution of the Electra complex twice, and with an Italian gardener at that, even if he is very handsome.

CHAPTER 4

Interview with Fred

Through our early childhood Susan was always the focus of attention; however, I shall tell you about a turn of events which led to me getting the spotlight for a while.

One morning I woke up feeling sick: my head buzzed, my knees ached, I had a pain in the stomach and spots all over. I crept into Mother's room and told her how awful I felt. She popped a thermometer into my mouth and carried me back to my own bed. When she discovered the thermometer read over one hundred she packed Susan off to school with a note about me, brought me some peppermint-tasting medicine and took my pulse. I felt very important and the whole household was very concerned about me. Mum stayed home from work and spent the morning reading stories and playing snakes and ladders with me. At lunch time Dad came home to see how I was and brought me a new set of colouring pencils. Aunty Ethel dropped in to visit and brought me some homemade chocolate cake and Mum produced some toys she had been saving for Christmas. By evening I had forgotten all my aches and pains. I had as much fun as though it were my birthday—more in fact, because I hadn't had to share it with Susan.

Next morning the prospect of going back to school was bleak, but to my relief Mother insisted I stay home for another day. In fact, when she mentioned it, I could feel all my symptoms returning. I passed another blissful day.

Two weeks later I was dreading school because of a spelling test for which I was unprepared. Mother thought I looked a little pale and asked whether I felt sick. I realised that my head was buzzing, my knees ached, I had a pain in the stomach and there were those spots all over me again. Susan grumblingly went off without me and I retreated to the comfort of a warm bed and lots of attention. Thereafter my illness struck from time to time and frequently coincided with term tests and sports days. Although my illnesses didn't interfere with Susan—in fact I enjoyed being away from her never-ending demands—she always seemed very put out when she came home from school and found me holding court in bed.

My continued illnesses worried my parents, who finally sent me to a specialist for a complete check-up and blood test. This of course was combined with a special treat because I was such a model patient during the examination. Mother, Father and doctor were all proud of me in turn. Only Susan was lacking in admiration and surreptitiously broke my favourite toy. In spite of the specialist's reassurances, my illnesses continued and, although Susan had been Queen of the Kindergarten, I became the Crown Prince at home.

My reign didn't go undisputed: I was threatened very soon by Susan's amateurish attempts at competition. The first round happened on the occasion of the next spelling test. I woke that morning with a buzzing head and red spots on my face which gave me a feeling of relief as the fear of the spelling test receded. When Mum left the room to get my usual pink medicine and breakfast in bed, Susan's face appeared above the blankets covered in bright red spots. As I was looking at her in astonishment and some chagrin, she let out a couple of heart-rending groans and appeared to faint back on her pillows. The sound effects brought Mum back in a hurry and my breakfast was forgotten as she turned white at the sight of Susan. Recovering slightly from the swoon, Susan was able to gasp out a list of symptoms which closely matched mine, except in intensity: hers were double mine, including the number of spots. The whole performance sickened me, and could only be considered wanton behaviour since Susan always got full marks for spelling. As we sat up side by side eating our breakfasts in bed, I realised my nice quiet day with Mother was ruined. Once more I was competing with Susan and, what's more, she was outdoing me.

After breakfast Susan's feverish tossing increased to such a pitch that Mother was in constant attendance on her, bringing her aspirin and sponging her face. Then a very strange thing happened: Susan's spots vanished. Mother's face was covered with amazement, mine with amusement! Mother made a quick dab at my spots (which stayed put) and then returned to confront Susan with the mirror. Somehow Susan's claim of a miracle cure didn't quite ring true after the discovery of a paint box under the pillow and Susan was smartly packed off to school, her promises of beatification for saintly healing failing to soften Mother. I lay back on my pillows with a sigh of relief.

Her later attempts gained slowly in sophistication and medical complexity and included aniseed balls in the cheeks which produced short-term mumps; a well-acted sprained ankle, which unfortunately refused to swell; an attack of sudden blindness which was frustrated by the sight of chocolate cake on a distant table; and three days when she twitched and jerked around the house leaving us all mystified until we found a bookmark in the Medical Dictionary at the entry on spasticity and pointed out to her that people were born with this condition, and that it wasn't catching. After this she took more pains with her medical research.

For quite a long time there was a remission of symptoms and Susan stayed healthy. I began to feel more secure and my own genuine symptoms, unspectacular though they were, remained undiagnosed and continued to receive respectful attention from the doctors.

As I was saying, Susan enjoyed good health for at least a year, and when she began to reject second helpings of puddings, this was at first ascribed to her developing consciousness of figure, consistent with increased preening in front of the mirror. But after a while we noticed that she ate less and less. Mother felt that if this was dieting, it was becoming excessive. Finally Susan would eat nothing except a scrap of bread. Mother and Father became really worried and I overheard discussions of "wasting disease" and anorexia nervosa. Meal times turned into sessions where Susan was continually coaxed to eat and promised rewards and outings in return. Our daily diet was dictated by Susan's erstwhile favourite dishes which Mother spent hours preparing. The doctors fussed around her although they were a little puzzled that while Susan was undeniably thinner, she wasn't the scarecrow that one would expect. The upheaval caused by Susan's "wasting disease" went on for months. Mother and Father were so anxious they lost weight themselves and in the end we were all on

After this she took more pains with her medical research

tonics. At school the girls all thought her condition interesting and very romantic and the teachers never scolded if she didn't do her homework.

The whole tragic affair came to an abrupt end with the "Chicken Incident". One night a whole roast chicken vanished from the kitchen pantry. Our large Afghan puppy was immediately suspected, chastised and banished to the back yard. Next morning on his return to the house, he made a beeline for Susan's bed. He scrambled under and emerged triumphant, dragging out a large white napkin containing the bare carcase of the said chicken and an applecore. No Afghan wraps the remains of his dinner quite so neatly so he was immediately exonerated. However, the case against Susan looked very black indeed. Confronted with the damaging evidence and the accusing dog, Susan eventually broke down. Over a four-course dinner (which she ate like a condemned person's last meal) she admitted that during all the months of not eating she had been sustained by a steady diet of hot dogs bought from her pocket money, supplemented by an occasional dog biscuit when the Afghan wasn't looking. At the rate of 3 hot dogs a day, 7 days a week for a period of 6 months, Susan had eaten 536 hot dogs of dubious quality—surely the average citizen's life share of this commodity and sufficient punishment in itself.

EXTRACT FROM MARIGOLD GOLEM'S DIARY

May 5

This is the third time in two months that Fred has had these spells of illness. Although I am worried about their cause, I really like to have him at home again for a few days at a time and to be able to fuss over him and shower him with affection. Trevor has also found the time to come home from the bank, which is quite unusual. However, I must analyse this situation without too much emotional ego involvement. If we can exclude physical illness altogether (and the regular coincidence of the episodes of illness with exams confirms this diagnosis), this leaves us with the alternatives of attention-getting behaviour or the possibility of an incipient galloping hypochondria.

However, this oversimplification is the trap that any psychiatrically naive medico would fall into. Careful interpretation of Volume II of Freud's *Collected Works* suggests that it is an unresolved dependency need (described as school-phobia by the unsophisticated lay analyst). In Fred's case this is brought about by periodic regressions to the oral stage with subsequent fixation. And I cannot but blame myself that this may be due to a flaw in the handling of toilet training, which I have already described. He is now striving to overcome deficiencies which developed much earlier.

August 10

Fred's illnesses seem to strengthen the bond between the twins. He waits eagerly for Susan to come home from school everyday. When he hears her footsteps on the stairs he becomes feverish with excitement, only to have a strong coughing spell when she enters the room. Susan seems quite worried about all this. When Fred was at the clinic the other day she accidentally broke one of his toys and was quite overcome with remorse all day, hiding behind a nervous giggle. I am quite apprehensive about the results of these tests; it is just possible that I have been wrong about the oral fixation and that there is a physical component in his illness. What a blot on my self-esteem that would be.

October 19

I have been very upset lately with Susan trying to fake sickness almost as if she were envious of Fred's illness, which I am sure is not so. It is simply overidentification with Fred, part of a normal defence mechanism. It is so difficult to observe the developing defence mechanisms and to decide when they are normal and when they shade into the abnormal.

January 15

Susan's condition is really much more serious than I was ready to admit. It is a full-blown case of anorexia nervosa. There is no definitive

Interview with Fred

explanation for its occurrence in so many young girls. A simple-minded explanation is that it is a case of identification with a slim pop singer or some other cultural heroine. I think the cause is more deep-seated than this. Nobody knows better than I that the prognosis for this illness is not good.

March 27

I should be very annoyed with Susan that she deceived us all with her "anorexia nervosa", but I am really relieved that it is nothing serious. Trevor thinks it is despicable for her to have lied and cheated like this and he wants to punish her severely. I must prevent this at all costs, it is quite natural for her to behave in this way in the context of a normal love-hate relationship. Punishment can only do harm by ruining her capacity for future love-hate relationships.

32   *Lost in the Freudian Forest*

Panther-in-Chief

CHAPTER 5

Interview with Susan

One evening after dinner, Mother and Father, with a solemn air, called us both into the living room. We went a little reluctantly, mentally calculating which of our most recent misdeeds had been discovered this time. But without much ado they announced that we were to spend our next long vacation at a very progressive holiday camp.

Camp Endeavour, we were told, was designed to expand our minds, harden our bodies and teach us some very important life skills. The overriding principle of the camp was community spirit, developed by living and sharing with peer groups; self-reliance and initiative were encouraged, and brotherly love, tolerance and freedom were the key words. The introduction to this humanistic outlook was to take place in a climate of fresh air, exercise and wholesome food at the cost of four hundred dollars per week per child. We got the impression that this was some sort of uneasy compromise in the continual tug-of-war between Mum's theories of child development and Dad's no-nonsense approach to growing-up tough.

Two weeks later we scrambled off the train at the nearest station to the camp and hiked twenty-four kilometres to the pearly gates of Camp Endeavour on the shores of Lake Hardship. Here we were met by a rugged individual in khaki shorts and football jersey who introduced herself as Panther-in-Chief, the camp mother to whom we could go with all our troubles. A junior Eagle then took us under his wing and that was the last we saw of the great white Panther until our departure, when she wrenched herself away from her cash register to wave us a cheery goodbye. The junior Eagle eyed us disparagingly, told Fred he was a toad (with which I agreed), told me I was a snake (which in all honesty wasn't so far off the mark) and then frog-marched us off to two different ex-army huts. The camp site had been left as natural as possible and the two huts rose from a sea of mud; the huts identical in their unpainted dreariness, distinguished only by a flag on one showing a green snake and on the other a brown toad.

Over the next few weeks we certainly learnt a lot of new skills which, although they may not have matched our parent's expectations, did in a way fulfill the camp prospectus. One might think all initiative would be stifled by the comprehensive set of rules which governed every moment of the day, but on the contrary, considerable innovation and ingenuity was developed by Fred and me to circumvent the rules without discovery.

To harden our bodies it was considered desirable for us to get up at 6.00 a.m., have a cold shower, march into the forest for a five-kilometre hike and to report back to the blockwarden, Little Eagle, by 8.00 a.m. On the other hand, it was considered bad form to force us to do this; modern educational psychologists consider it important that these activities should be motivated by an inner need. In order to develop this inner need, the authorities allocated six points for completing the circuit each day. Thirty-six points earned a wooden shield for the week and four such shields could be exchanged for a golden toad or snake made from brass at the end of the camp holiday. It was surprising how many of our camp mates fell for this cheap psychological ruse and it became almost embarrassing for Fred and me to be lolling in our beds until breakfast time fulfilling an inner need which was very strong in us. It slowly became obvious to our brain-washed little camp mates that instead of being mortified at our bankruptcy in points and shields, we were looking pretty smug and living a much more comfortable life than they were. They could not understand that we merely had a different value system in which shields and brass toads figured not at all, and they kept pestering us to tell them our secret. So we invented the Susan and Fred (SF) antisuffering point system. The principle was the same as that used by the camp authorities, but the outcome was much more pleasant. If you stayed in bed until 8 a.m. you got six SF points, after a week this was converted into a PC (physical comfort) point and at the end of camp you were awarded the MM (maturity medal). In true Zen buddhist tradition

Interview with Susan

all these points were internalised, which means simply that they were imaginary and you did not have to recycle any wooden shields or give away silly brass tokens. It was based on the principle that two hours in a warm bed are more rewarding than cold showers and long walks, and that therefore the inner need to be comfortable will develop faster than the need to keep your body healthy through prolonged minor abuse. Our method was most satisfactory and all our hut mates joined in this new game except for the block warden. The shower-walk cycle was unsupervised—rather than get up himself at 6.00 a.m. the block warden had instituted an "honour system". Since no one bothered to tell him otherwise, he assumed they were still competing fiercely for points and he continued to award wooden shields every week. This meant that our followers really got the best of both worlds— inner harmony and a brass ornament.

There were other systems of self-discipline which developed into a real Catch 22. We were required to wash our socks every night, dry them and lay them out at right angles to the top of the bed, for inspection every morning. Compliance with this routine was rewarded by a parcel of camp-made cookies which were even more inedible than the rest of the camp food. Now it was really not taxing to conform to the sock ritual, but it was difficult to escape the consequences of the cookie reward. If you ate them they came to rest like stones in your stomach. If they were found in your possession it meant a punishment, usually withdrawal of the privilege of going to the movies which was the only tolerable activity in the camp routine. We tried feeding them to the goats of a neighbourhood farmer, but even they refused this treat. Some of our friends started burying them and thus escaped punishment. This would have been an admirable solution to the problem, but the cookies were unearthed from their shallow graves by camp rats, who also refused to eat them. They started to pile up around the camp site and began to arouse the suspicion of Eagles and Panthers. They believed we were raiding the pantry for their cookie treasures and posted night guards in the kitchen compound. Then it occurred to Fred that we could simply stop participating in the sock routine. It would solve all problems inherent in the present cookie disposal scheme and avoid punishment. No clean socks—no cookies —no punishment and everybody could enjoy the movies. It worked

They started to pile up around the camp site

Interview with Susan

because the camp authorities could not retract their principle of making us do things by voluntary means, using extrinsic rewards or punishments only for initial guidance. Eventually they rationalised that the subtle rejection of the unwholesome cookies was a result of their daily lectures on "healthy" eating and that we had been converted to better dental hygiene by giving up an undesirable sugar intake. Thus their honour was saved, and among our fellow sufferers our prestige increased even further.

Another objectionable routine designed to foster team spirit and healthy competition was the Route March. We were divided into two groups for this purpose, the Hawks and the Rabbits, each consisting of both girls and boys. This cut across the Toad-Snake division which was strictly sexist—Toads being male and Snakes being female. Every second day after breakfast these two groups set out across the countryside with a map, to rendezvous eleven kilometres on the other side of the little town near our camp. The group that arrived first would plant its flag there and return to camp as the winner. This group was allowed to host the feast on Saturday night at which both the winners and the losers shared the only decent meal of the camp week. Both groups attended and toasted each other with lemonade. This ritual was designed to further the team spirit and make us "good losers". Fred and I could see no point in a twenty-two kilometre cross-country run when nothing was gained except a hollow victory (or hollow defeat, as the case may be). We soon spotted the local bus which passed along the road not far from our meeting place at the other end of town. It was child's play to obtain a timetable and work out a routine which provided for Hawks and Rabbits to catch a bus to the rendezvous spot, picnic there on our own food purchased in town and unbelievably superior to the camp hash, spend a comfortable hour or two playing cards or dominoes and return on another bus to town. We drew lots for winners and the winners were given a two-minute start from the bus stop to return to camp while the losers returned to camp panting for the last hundred metres. Both groups of course had to roll in the mud to look like tough route marchers. Panther-in-Chief was delighted with our exhibition of unfaltering team competition and our noble example of losing without showing any bitterness. Although we did not see her face to face, rumours reached us that we were the best

Lost in the Freudian Forest

Communication is consciousness-raising

group Camp Endeavour had ever housed.
We returned home very satisfied with the camp holiday. It had been a good training ground to foster our initiative and self-reliance without the serious discomforts of Camp Endeavour's usual "tough" routine and we had succeeded in helping the camp authorities to maintain their delusional system. At home, we thought the matter over and decided our parents might as well be left with their delusions too, since there were no other children in our family who could come to grief in such a camp if they arrived there with less initiative.

Letter from Trevor Golem to his brother Bert

Dear Bert,
 I hope that you and your family are well and content. Lately I have been thinking of you very often because Marigold and I have been facing many problems in the upbringing of the twins. As you are aware, we don't always agree on methods of child rearing. Marigold believes in Freudian methods and I am entirely a man of the old school, in favour of strict discipline and acceptance of old-fashioned values, and I think that her methods are often extraordinary.
 But now I think that we have come to a turning point and I believe that my insistence on some discipline has at last paid off. The twins have spent this summer vacation at Camp Endeavour, a place designed to encourage self-reliance, initiative and brotherly love. In other words, a place where the old-fashioned values, in which both you and I believe, are still being fostered. Two days ago Fred and Susan returned from their vacation, suntanned and happy, but not very talkative about their experiences. I did not question them since I do not believe in this continuous new-fangled "communication" where everybody says everything to everybody else so that they get to know each other and themselves better. Of course, Marigold was not happy about the silence since she says communication is consciousness-raising and essential to the growing-up process.
 However, my chance to find out without pestering the twins came yesterday at the bank, when I met the father of one of the other boys who had been at Camp Endeavour. He congratulated me on Fred and Susan, and said that his boy told him that they were the life and

joy of the camp, and heroes to all the children because they had made it a bearable place for all the others. Needless to say, I was very proud of them, and I know now that my insistence on retaining some of the old values has been more than justified.

I want you and Mabel to know the good news since you are the only ones aware of my struggle at home. I also want to tell you, Bert, that I feel now the twins are ready to accept your long-standing invitation to visit during the next vacation. You will be able to add to the good work which was begun this year at the camp.

With best regards
and brotherly love

Trevor

EXTRACT FROM MARIGOLD GOLEM'S DIARY

August 30

Two days ago the twins returned from Camp Endeavour. They are so grown-up, but have hardly spoken about the camp. For the first time, I have been unable to communicate with them and to get to know their inner life. This could be very dangerous. I hope that I will be able to erase the effects of this authoritarian camp in the next few weeks. I am sure I have laid good foundations for their future psychic adjustment and I pray to Freud that my good work with them will prevail.

CHAPTER 6

Interview with Fred

The year after the summer vacation in camp our parents decided that a simple country holiday would be an invaluable experience for us. So one sunny summer's morning we were packed off by train to spend the vacation with Uncle Bert, Auntie Mabel and the cousins. Of course, we had met them all before when they visited town for the annual shopping spree but we didn't know them as well as Mum's sister, Aunty Ethel, who had done some surreptitious spoiling of us in our youth. In spite of a fleeting acquaintance with this country branch of the family, we were quite unaware of what we might find out there in the bush. Any place away from our school crowd seemed a dull prospect to us, since we would miss our attentive audience whom we had recently started educating in Mother's psychoanalytic literature. But perhaps we could kindle this interest in our cousins too.

Uncle Bert was not only a farmer but also a methodist lay preacher and, as Mother told us at the railway station, a good and righteous man but very different from our father. She did not elaborate on this statement and we drew our own not very flattering conclusions. We were also told that Auntie Mabel was a fine woman who had given birth to eight children, of whom only six had survived.

At the railway station cousins Ted and Abigail collected us in their own jalopy and we were impressed that our two older cousins were grown-up enough to have driver's licences. We brightened up at the prospect of having at least two kindred souls around us, since the other cousins were small vermin, all aged less than ten.

At the homestead we were welcomed by the rest of the family, barking sheepdogs, and tea and scones in the front parlour. The farmhouse was old and homely and we were struck by the large number

Uncle Bert

Interview with Fred

of hand-embroidered mottos which adorned every wall. The two most memorable were a large green floral one facing the toilet seat which read "Hardships build character" and below that a multicoloured one with "per ardua ad astra".

Uncle laid down the household routine for us without further ado. First: rise at 5.30 a.m. Each pronouncement was followed by a question on our part, since our parents had encouraged us to ask the why's and what's about everything. I don't think Uncle felt the same way about it, since he started to look a trifle irritated after the first couple of questions. I remember that first conversation very clearly. It went like this:

> Uncle: In this house we get up early. I expect you out of bed at 5.30 every morning including Sundays.
> Susan: That's a bit early. Do you want us to help with the milking?
> Uncle: Don't be silly—you'd only frighten the cows dry. [He pointed at the motto above the door.] "Early to bed, early to rise makes you healthy, wealthy and wise"—and even if you don't get any wiser, it's good for you.

And then he went on with the routine.

> Uncle: You must have a cold shower before breakfast, which is at 5.45.
> Susan: Isn't there any hot water so early in the morning?
> Uncle: Yes, there is hot water all day but this is how Christ showered himself and it will build your characters. Before breakfast you take two tablespoons of Epsom salts.
> Susan: Why? We are never constipated and Mother asks us about our motions every day.
> Uncle: This has nothing to do with your bowel movements—it is the best way to cleanse the inner man or woman. Your aunt and I have followed this practice for thirty-five years and look at us.

We looked at them and saw a worn-out, prematurely aged couple and remained totally unimpressed. By that time I think Uncle had lost his patience and the conversation came to a halt. Now, after many years, the picture is perfectly clear and Mum's parting remark also falls into place. Uncle and Aunt were totally devoted to the principle that "whatever is unpleasant is bound to be good for you" and this was manifested in many ways other than early rising, cold showers and Epsom salts. Thus we were given columns and columns of figures to add every day—not to help Uncle with his bookkeeping but to

44 *Lost in the Freudian Forest*

A cold shower before breakfast

Interview with Fred

keep our "mathematical muscles" flexed. Or we dug a large hole in the backyard only to fill it the next day—not in order to plant something, oh no, but "to remain at one with nature". The worst part was compulsory attendance at Uncle's sermons twice every Sunday and a few more, off the cuff, in the dining room during the week. On top of all this, Aunt Mabel provided wholesome badly cooked food, spiced only with prayers, and the Bible was the only book in the house.

The absence of books was not remarkable. Uncle was thoroughly committed to practical matters—he could understand only what he could touch, hear and see. Even his Christianity was practical: God was considered as a kind of merchant and one had to pay for what one received. His credo was that mental health (by which we can only assume he meant "satisfaction for the psyche") could be achieved by the principle that regular exercise ensures a sound mind in a sound body. In contrast, our mother's approach to life was based on a comprehensive psychoanalytic framework where satisfaction for the psyche comes from the recognition and acceptance of sexual problems and a frank approach to their solution. Her great wisdom in this regard was based on years of wide reading of the best theoreticians. What hope for Abigail and Ted, growing up in a house with only one book.

One rainy day after we had done justice to Uncle's character-building exercise by two hours of chopping wood in the driving rain and becoming thoroughly drenched, we were allowed to retire to the attic. This seemed a good opportunity to broaden our cousins' horizons and to tell them about some of Mum's recent theories. Susan proceeded to explain about infant sexuality and eroticism, while I emphasised the importance of discarding the earlier forms of sexual gratification in favour of more mature ones and the difficulties encountered with the resolution of the Oedipus and Electra complexes. At first they looked a little blank and then expressed astonishment by forgetting to shut their mouths. Obviously they were quite nonplussed and did not understand what we were talking about. Moreover they were not the admiring audience with avid questions that our city friends provided when we held forth on these topics. Their only response was to suggest a game of "snakes and ladders". By supper time it seemed we had settled down to an amicable but dull relationship.

After being sent to bed at 7.00 p.m., Susan and I felt rather hungry after the unpalatable supper of dry bread and boiled vegetables. We decided to sneak down to the kitchen and knock up a couple of ham and cheese sandwiches. Salivating at the thought of these delicacies we were at the top of the stairs when we heard Uncle say:

"We have been visited by the devil. Fred and Susan are going to destroy the innocence and Godliness of our children with their filthy talk about infantile sexuality. If Ted had not come and asked us whether he had demonstrated an Oedipus complex we would have never known about this corruption. I told them both not to talk to Fred and Susan about these horrible things anymore, and should they start again, to turn the conversation to the Bible."

We snuck back to bed, hungry and dejected.

Next day was a beautiful sunny day and we felt more in harmony with our surroundings as the four of us walked around the paddocks. The peaceful scene of quietly grazing cattle was suddenly broken by a huge bull violently attacking a cow from behind. We were afraid the poor cow would be hurt but could do nothing to help. It was a frightening sight and we expected Ted and Abigail to run for help. The cousins, however, seemed entirely unconcerned, so we asked them why they were doing nothing to separate the two animals. When they realised our question was serious, they reacted by rolling in the paddock with laughter. When they calmed down, Ted asked me whether I didn't really know what these animals were doing. When he explained, we were flabbergasted. Susan told me later that she felt positively sick. She could not imagine that sex was so ugly and violent. Our first reaction was that Freud could never have known what was going on at these farms—and in the name of God.

It was only that evening that the full shock hit us, when we realised from our theoretical knowledge that the same procedure must apply to humans.

For the rest of the week we had to refuse offers from Ted and Abigail to take us on other farm excursions to further our education. At the weekend our decision to return to the city was greeted with relief by our uncle and aunt, and with smug looks from the cousins.

Letter from Bert Golem to his brother Trevor

August 30

Dear Trevor,

It is with a heavy heart that I write to you today, but I feel it is my duty to be the sender of bad news. As pleased as I was with your letter last year telling me of the twins' success at camp, their stay with us was a dismal failure.

From the very first day here, they questioned all my demands and the rules of our household. Then they tried to poison the minds of the children and undo my teaching of Ted and Abigail by talking about filth and perversion. Fortunately, my own innocent children were guided by God to seek me out immediately and tell me of these shameful goings-on. I absolutely forbade any mention of these topics in my house and the name of Freud stands henceforth banned in this part of the world, as was Darwin's in Pennsylvania for many decades. It was God's will and I neither questioned Him nor the twins when they cut their visit short. It seemed our strict adherence here to a simple morality was too much for them. Trevor, as a brother and a man of God, I must urge you to take the upbringing of your children into firmer hands. I pray that God will help you in this and that you shall remain strong with such evil in the house.

Yours,

Bert

EXTRACT FROM MARIGOLD GOLEM'S DIARY

August 30

The twins returned unexpectedly early from their vacation on the farm. They were upset and quite confused. When I pieced things together, it appeared that the crude copulating of farm animals had shocked their sensitive psyches.

The name of Freud stands henceforth banned in this part of the world

Perhaps it was a mistake in having kept sex education for them on a theoretical level, without allowing them exposure to the more mechanistic and practical side

Perhaps it was a mistake in having kept sex education for them on a theoretical level, without allowing them exposure to the more mechanistic and practical side. They probably know more about Freud's theory of psychosexual development than any other children their age. I thought the most progressive way of approaching the problem was to play down the seedy side of it. I hope it is not too late to do something to fill the gap.

Unfortunately, the children's request for further information took the form of asking me and Trevor to demonstrate the primal scene. Even if Trevor had not refused point blank, I didn't know what to say myself. Dear me, what would Freud do? I'm sure he didn't walk around the house naked!

CHAPTER 7

Interview with Susan

Mother believed very strongly that one should like to do things for their own sake, including cooking, housework, playing music; I am not sure whether she drew the line at cleaning the toilet. She also believed, and this was based on the theory of a man called Allport, that this liking can be developed over time. At first you carry out some activity, say brushing your teeth, to please your mother or for some other reward. After a while you get to like it for its own sake and in some cases you become addicted to it, so that with regard to cleaning your teeth you either become a compulsive who carries a whole range of toothbrushes in your handbag or you become a successful dentist. It was not unlike one of the principles which we demolished at Camp Endeavour, only Mother was a good deal more sophisticated about it. She called it "functional autonomy" for the sake of this guy Allport. She was particularly insistent on this "pleasure through perseverence" with regard to the piano.

Ever since I can remember, I had piano lessons once a week from Mrs Sebastian. She was an old dear, positively ancient, wrinkled and badly crippled by neuralgia; sometimes bad tempered, but on the whole quite nice. She tried to teach me music reading, finger exercises, simple songs and Beethoven. My progress was very slow and instead of getting to like it, I got to hate it. Even Mrs Sebastian began to lose her temper with me and sometimes rapped my fingers with her pencil, which didn't really hurt but was rather humiliating. I kept waiting for the moment when the magic change predicted by Mother would occur—I was really quite patient about it. I even practised when I had nothing else to do. I knew things would be much easier when the change came, but nothing happened, and one day just before my fourteenth birthday, when Mum asked what I wanted as a birthday present I said, without hesitation, "I want to stop having piano lessons". Mum was quite taken back, Dad laughed hilariously and after a while Mother pleaded with me to continue for another year. She looked so pathetic when she said "try it for my sake" that I agreed, although I knew it was not for her sake but for that guy Allport's sake.

Shortly after my birthday, poor old Mrs Sebastian got too ill to continue and there was a three-week respite in piano lessons. On the fourth Thursday when I walked into the room to resume piano lessons, I was dumbstruck. Instead of Mrs Sebastian there was this gorgeous young man sitting on the piano stool. I first thought I was dreaming one of the better known fairytales, where the ugly old witch is turned into a beautiful young prince, usually through the kiss of an innocent maiden. I would have given anything to be the young maiden myself, except of course I was not really innocent. Eric from 2b had been my steady now for three months, carrying my school books and holding my hand when nobody was looking. The young god introduced himself as Adonis Sebastian, Mrs Sebastian's nephew, and informed me that he would continue as my piano teacher in his aunt's place. I was quite confounded by this news and for the first time in my life I had nothing to say. I was too scared to speak, in case he turned back into a frog. From then on I applied myself to the piano with great earnestness. During lessons I hardly spoke at all and concentrated on doing exactly what he wanted, at least for the first few lessons until I got some of my courage back. I also practised endlessly and Mother had a smile on her face—she was certain her theory was beginning to work. I must confess I adored Adonis from the beginning. He probably thought I was rather shy and perhaps silly, the way I behaved, unable to put three words together. Then I began to see little signs that made me think it might have been love at first sight for him too. He was so gentlemanly and considerate: he turned the music for me, sometimes he touched my hands pretending that it was accidental. Or he held my hand just a little longer than necessary when he showed me how to reach an octave. A couple of times our knees touched when he moved closer with eagerness for my piano playing. He sometimes asked me to brush the hair out of my eyes; when I did so, and looked into his eyes, there was fire in his glance. One day he gave me a lift

Interview with Susan

Adonis Sebastian

in his car and although I sat in the backseat with two other girls, I felt he was driving only for me. His most open declaration of love was when he lent me his biography of Tschiakowsky. I understood the message he wanted me to know: our own romance was so beautifully depicted in this book. This bliss continued for many weeks. I trembled and blushed when we met, and could hardly keep my hands from shaking when I played for him. I felt the whole world must know, but nobody seemed to notice because Adonis was so discreet. And I began to enjoy the piano more than anything else in life—for the first time I knew what functional autonomy was—my mother was right, the piano had become the joy of my life.

I also knew where my duty lay with regard to my old boyfriend Eric. I wrote to him that we must break up. I implored him to be civilised about it, not to commit suicide, to try and get over the tragedy and to cherish our brief time together in his memory. There was no reason why, by the age of thirty, he might not meet and marry another woman, perhaps a well-preserved widow who would be the solace of his old age and console him for losing me. It was the only honest thing to do under the circumstances, and I did it.

My affair with Adonis continued: secret hand touches, long lingering looks—always that feeling of togetherness, love and belongingness, expressed in so many small ways which only I could understand.

Then one day he took the inevitable step. He proposed an elopement. Of course not in a crude way, but very subtly, by suggesting that we meet at the railway station to go jointly to the Eistedfodd for which we had been practising for months. I knew immediately what the real purpose was, I felt naive that I had misinterpreted the preparation for the Eistedfodd simply as part of his duty as a music teacher, when all the time it had been a well-planned operation for us to be together and eventually join in holy wedlock. It was a romantic plan, typical of Adonis' brilliant intellect and irresistible charm. On the appointed day I packed a case with nightgowns, my best underwear, Mother's French perfume and my favourite doll. Before going to Mum's beauty parlour to prepare for the great event, I wrote a note to Dad explaining everything: about my passionate affair with Adonis that had flowered over the last few months, as well as our intended elopement. I thought he would understand, he had a romantic vein.

Interview with Susan 55

When I went home to collect my case, with only little time to reach the station at the appointed hour, there was bedlam. Dad had come home from the bank in the middle of the day (an unheard-of event), after my letter had been opened by his nosey assistant manager. I heard later that the whole bank staff had been full of pity for Dad, because they thought the letter was from Marigold and all this had occurred in the presence of an inspector from Head Office. Dad was in a state of great excitement. He asked me if it were true—and of course I had to confirm it, although I could see that losing his daughter was breaking his heart. He grabbed me by the hand, almost knocking off my new eyelashes, dragged me into the car and drove at great speed to the station. I was still full of joy, in spite of being sorry for Dad, and angry that he had left my suitcase behind. I knew when he saw me with Adonis everything would be well.

At the entrance of the station I saw my lover towering over the crowd and I managed to break away from Dad. Adonis was looking my way, his eyes only for me, and his lips moving in silent prayer. But when I managed to push my way through the crowd, my world crashed to ruins about me. I found him not praying, but counting twenty little girls, everyone of them clutching music and suitcases and everyone of them en route to the Eistedfodd. Dad seemed magically to calm down, smilingly kissed me goodbye and promised to send my suitcase on the next train. But I, with my heart breaking, my romance shattered, had to suffer in silence with twenty chattering schoolgirls, and my hero paying equal attention to all of them.

EXTRACT FROM MARIGOLD GOLEM'S DIARY

February 3

Susan seems unable to develop the love for music which I expected would occur after perseverance with piano lessons—I was rather disappointed when she asked to be allowed to stop lessons as a birthday present. I think she was trying to tell me that I must look for an alternative way to instil this intrinsic motive to play the piano. I am sure she really wants to learn, and I cannot imagine I am projecting my own desires on her. I was particularly careful with regard to her early environment: even during my pregnancy I played classical music every day. Latest scientific findings confirm what some of the farsighted psychoanalysts have always maintained: that prenatal environment is all important to character formation. In fact some theorists date the beginning of this influence to the day of conception. During the twins' infancy they were continuously exposed to music's three B's. I think it is right to persuade her to continue; the love for music must come any moment now.

February 28

I knew it all the time. There has been a sudden change in Susan's attitude to the piano. She practises every free moment now. She plays new pieces even if they sound atrocious, and listens to the record player with great rapture. It cannot be the new teacher, he is much too young and inexperienced to bring about such a profound change. It is just coincidence that he and the breakthrough of functional autonomy arrived at the same time. Susan has reached that particular stage in her development which I have predicted. Her maturity seems to generalise to other behaviour too. She smiles more and is pleasant to everybody and takes more care of her personal appearance. She admires herself in front of the mirror trying new hairdos, and I haven't seen her in jeans for weeks. Yesterday she even asked me how much my beauty treatments cost and whether she could have one some day soon. I suppose it is all part of the growing-up process. I must be more patient in the future and not lose faith too soon, in particular when I know these things follow a well-ordered pattern.

March 10

I was not at all surprised when I heard the story of Susan's crush on the piano teacher. It was part of her greater maturity which I described two weeks ago, and Adonis is such an adorable-looking man that any woman could fall in love with him. Trevor, of course, was in a state of old-fashioned fatherly rage until he realised it was all Susan's imagination. And there was some unpleasantness at his work

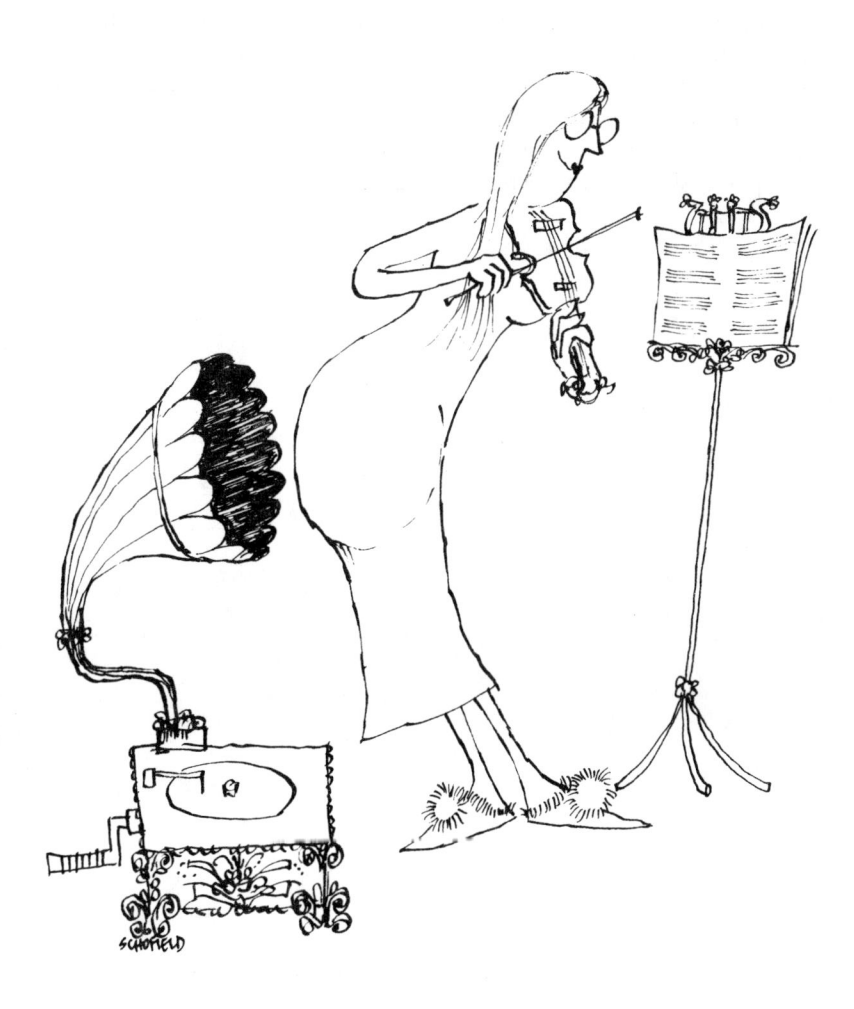

Even during my pregnancy I played classical music every day

over Susan's letter. Really, they are a very inhibited, repressed group of people in that bank. The elopement was part of her healthy fantasy life which is an essential part of everybody's psychosexual development. The only worry I have about this episode is that Adonis Sebastian is so unlike Trevor. I wonder whether this shows a worrying absence of identification with her real father, almost like the absence of an Electra complex. As Freud would say, in Adonis she chose an unsuitable object for a suitable emotion.

Since all is resolved now, my only concern is that her love for the piano should survive the trauma.

CHAPTER 8

Interview with Fred

One of my earliest memories of Dad is his talk about a "good" school and the importance of wearing the right school tie. At first it didn't mean very much to me, but later I understood that Dad saw himself as a self-made man who had not had the right educational opportunities as a child and who had to struggle very hard to achieve his present position in the bank. It was clear that Dad wanted me to grow up without having to face any of the disadvantages which he himself had had to face as a youngster. Sometimes he became very vocal about the role of school ties and the old-boy network in the building of a career. I used to sit at his feet and listen to exciting stories of life in the Great Public Schools: the noble sportsmen of the playing field, the heroes of cricket, the communal team spirit culminating in victories at the regatta; the slow build-up with fagging, cold showers, frugal meals and other character training which eventually makes a fully fledged member of this most desirable society, for whom all doors are open all the time. The tough side of the early part of this life was well outweighed by the gains in prestige, the elegance and graciousness of their homelife. I often wondered about Dad's detailed knowledge of Great Public School life until I discovered the *Boy's Own Annual* and *Tom Brown's School Days*. The glamour of these schools was firmly fixed in my mind and not long after I turned fifteen, I was thrilled when Father informed me that I was to leave State School at the end of the year because I had been accepted as a student in St Malcolm's College, the finest school in our city.

However, with the shopping preparations prior to the commencement of the school year, under Dad's personal supervision, I became slightly apprehensive. The influx of school uniforms included straw

The milk bar

Interview with Fred

boaters, ties and socks to match. My first lounge suit at the age of fifteen, white shirts and even a tuxedo, gave me a feeling of unreality and a fear that I may not be able to live up to Dad's expectations. I also felt regretful that I had to leave my easy-going friends with their patched jeans, tee shirts and sneakers. I was afraid I would miss their easy-going ways and way-out music and finish up a polished snob listening to classical music, when at heart I was a lazy slob without any great ambitions, not at all like my sister Susan. Maybe she should have been the boy, but meanwhile I had to shoulder the burden and try to help fulfill Dad's ambitions—so when he gave me lessons from Nancy Mitford's book I dropped all my "non U sayings" in favour of a vocabulary that would have done justice to the English peerage.

The first week at St Malcolm's was a great effort. We were all dressed alike, immaculate in our blazers and striped school ties. But I felt stiff and solemn, overdressed and constantly saying the wrong things. The other boys were polite to me, rude to each other, laughing at a lot of "in" jokes and less than friendly to me. For the first few weeks I coasted along as a loner, not making any friends and sneaking back to my old haunt, in particular the milk bar where my State School friends used to meet in the afternoon. Here I had to endure their friendly teasing about my posh school suit and polished shoes, but to be back in their company was worth it.

My seat at St Malcolm's was next to William Torpington-Smith who was polite enough to me; but on the whole he ignored my presence, although he seemed to be ring leader of the smartest set in my class. I was therefore surprised and totally unprepared when he invited me to a little "shindig" at his place on the following Saturday night. I rushed home and told Dad about our good fortune. He got very excited and told me what a fine family the Torpington-Smiths were, amongst the wealthiest customers of his bank. We debated whether I should wear the tuxedo or the lounge suit on this occasion and Dad felt since it was the beginning of term and there was no written invitation, I should settle for the suit. He gave me elaborate hints on how to deal with the butler and to be sure to address the parents as "madam" and "sir" and to watch and see whether the other boys left tips for the maid. In fact he told me to have some small change ready for just such an emergency.

He gave me elaborate hints on how to deal with the butler and to be sure to address the parents as "madam" and "sir"

Interview with Fred 63

I set off in the full glamour of new suit with new shirt, tie, socks and shoes, turned out to a tee. I stepped out with great bravado as a man of the world that I knew pleased Dad, but inwardly I was apprehensive. I felt the occasion was to be a test for me, to see if I were worthy to join the inner circle at St Malcolms—but I was not sure what form it would take. Since it was early, I strolled around the neighbourhood keeping my eyes on the front door of the T.-S.'s mansion. I was astonished to see a group of four or five boys enter dressed in jeans with thongs on their feet. Since I was a long way down the street I did not recognise any of their faces and hid in the bushes nextdoor to the house to make sure it was the right place. Soon I was surprised and delighted to see some of my class mates going into the house all dressed in the scruffiest of jeans, without coats, and with sandals or thongs on their feet. I rushed home, quietly entered our back yard and threw a pebble at Susan's window. When she opened the window, I whispered to her to get my jeans and tee shirt and within three minutes I clutched a bundle of clothes in my hands. The change in the toolshed was accomplished in the dark to avoid drawing my parent's attention to my return home. Soon I was standing in front of the T.-S.'s door ringing the bell. William, wearing paint-spattered jeans, opened the door for me. There were no butler, parents or maid in sight. He ushered me into a large room with furniture carelessly pushed to the wall and the whole mob sitting on the floor, drinking cokes and munching hamburgers and chips, and listening to some groovy records. They nodded to me and for the first time since I had come to St Malcolm's I felt at ease. It was just the sort of party my friends at the State School would throw. I dropped all my new polish and enjoyed myself greatly. I knew I had been accepted when T.-S. agreed to swap records with me. Going home I was floating on a cloud; life was going to be bearable. But somehow I felt I had to protect Dad from my new discovery. I changed back into my spotless party clothes in the dark toolshed and as I entered through the front door I saw Dad in the sitting room with his bank ledger and a pencil. He was pretending to work, but I knew that he was really waiting up to hear all about our first party. I didn't let him down; everything had been just as he had described it to me. I fed him back his own story embroidered with pieces from my imagination and my own

Lost in the Freudian Forest

It was just the sort of party my friends at the State School would throw

wide reading of the *Boy's Own Paper*. Both of us went to bed truly happy: I because I could face the future at St Malcolm's, and he because all his hopes for me had come true.

My double life continued in much the same way for the next two years. Dad saw the school only on speech days and sports days, with all the veneer in its place: boys well behaved in their immaculate school uniforms, calling teachers and fathers "sir". This image was supplemented by my stories of grand parties at the Torpington-Smith's, Huntington-Chorea's and Tasmania-Sach's (known as Tay to his friends) and with the offspring of other important families that numbered amongst Dad's most distinguished customers. My acceptance by the gang and my father's fantasies about the nature of their life were both maintained without a flaw. One difficulty was avoiding Father's eager offer to throw a party at home in return for all the hospitality I had received. This offer included a hired butler, footmen, maids and crockery and cutlery. Only my expertise at stalling and inventing imaginary illnesses for my friends (I dared not fake illness myself) prevented the disaster. My opportunity for a good party with the usual trimmings at our place came when my parents and Susan were out of town—a practice followed and understood by all my friends.

Occasionally there was a close shave when Dad saw me with my scruffy friends in a downtown record shop or milk bar. He always mistook them for the State School mob and chided me for keeping up this contact, adding that he was certain that my new friends wouldn't approve of my old proletarian associates.

All went well, until one day at a lively party at the T.-S.'s we decided to gate-crash a party given by one of the girls from our sister school, St Renata. We entered en masse, swigging coke from king-size bottles and were shocked to find the girl's parents were home. They failed to recognise the scions from such great fraternal families and called the police.

There we were, lined up at the Police Station waiting for our parents to deliver us from the clutches of the Law. Dad arrived first, shocked to find me with such companions, convinced that I had fallen into the evil ways of the State School mob again. I am not sure whether he was even more shocked when all his star customers arrived to collect

Lost in the Freudian Forest

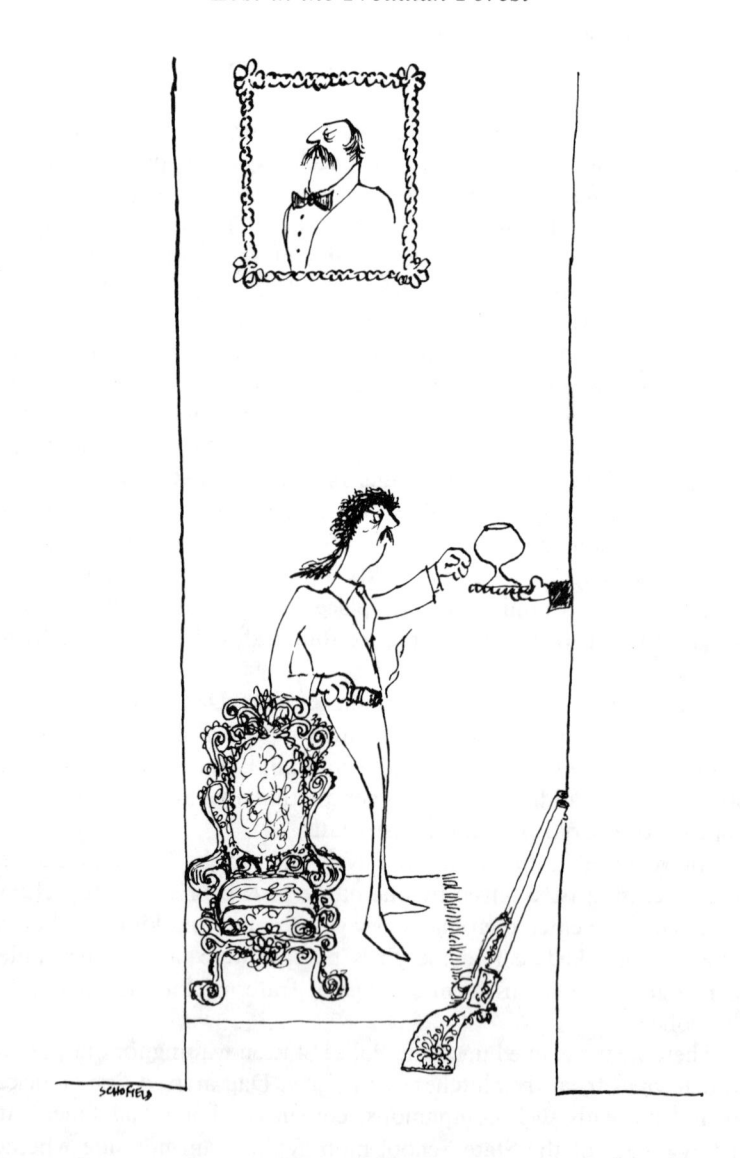

The Huntington-Chorea's

their own offspring, or whether he felt reassured that I had at least been in good company. I never found out: we didn't discuss the matter and my stories about the prestigeful school and my friends ceased abruptly. The disappointment must have been very hard on Dad and he withdrew more and more into his bank vaults.

EXTRACT FROM MARIGOLD GOLEM'S DIARY

May 2

Lately Trevor and Fred have had so many earnest conversations, not really secretive, but in a sort of private man-to-man style. From the bits I could overhear without appearing to be eavesdropping, there is a new affinity between them, a very comradely relationship. Obviously a rapid resolution of the Oedipus complex has taken place. It seems a complete justification of my method and Father Freud would be proud of me, if he is watching up there over the doings of his disciples. He said that this is one of the most difficult barriers in the child-rearing process. He was less lucid than usual in his prescriptions of how to handle this oedipal situation and I think I detect a note of pessimism in his writing on that subject. Perhaps a painless transition like the Trevor-Fred one which I have just witnessed would have been impossible in the unenlightened Society of Vienna in the early twentieth century. Maybe I have engineered a breakthrough and have a right to give my name to this bond. I must raise this at the next Psychoanalytic Congress. Surely this is more important than the "fear of flying" which came out of the last one.

May 17

These all-male sessions between Fred and Trevor really are becoming a trifle adolescent. Fred is beginning to identify completely with the Bank Manager image and his mode of dress and clichés are very middle class. I wasn't too pleased to hear that Fred has been accepted into St Malcolm's next term. Trevor has been arguing for this for some time and he must have used all the influence he could

68   *Lost in the Freudian Forest*

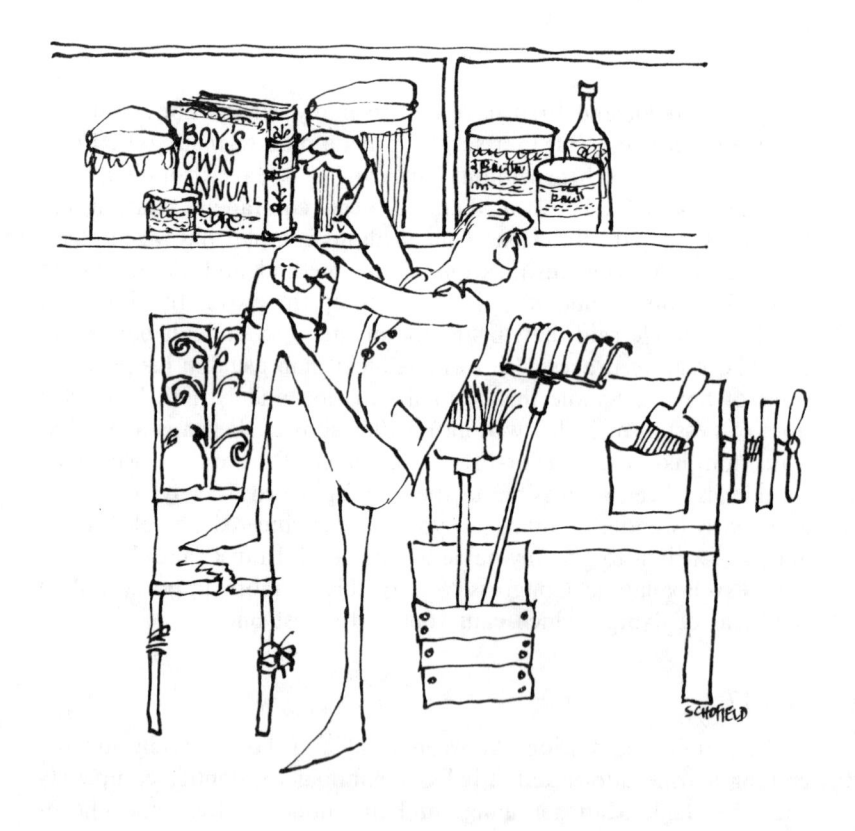

An extreme form of emotional laziness

Interview with Fred 69

Trevor has been seriously withdrawn

bring to bear to get Fred into the school. However, I cannot put up any opposition: the new "Marigold bond" between them is the most important thing (that phrase does sound good, maybe it will be accepted world-wide one day).

September 20

Fred has now been at St Malcolm's for nearly two years. I think I was misguided to permit such a retrogressive step in Fred's educational programme. The school promotes snobbism and all this dressing-up with emphasis on materialistic things is just sickening decadence. His best friends now come from that pompous crowd of the Torpington-Smiths, and other nouveaux riches. I can see through Trevor quite clearly; he wants to relive his own childhood through Fred. This is really an extreme form of emotional laziness. He is using Fred quite unashamedly to promote his own fantasy life. It is so unfair to Fred to have pulled him out of his old environment and furthermore to alienate him from his mother. And worse still, Fred seems to have fallen for all this; he is a changed person. I am at a loss to know what to do about it. I feel like the sorcerer's apprentice who has released the floods and cannot stop them. I am afraid it is getting too much for me. I seem to have lost all influence with Fred. Maybe there are some serious drawbacks in the "Marigold bond".

October 2

This is the first breakthrough in months. I am glad those St Malcolm's boys showed some healthy spunk in indulging in a bit of anti-authoritarian gate-crashing and finding Fred a ring-leader in this makes me hopeful again. I know this seems unfair to Trevor and I am sorry. Trevor has been seriously withdrawn in the last few day. He could have a schizophrenic breakdown anytime. I must bide my satisfaction at the new turn of events and pretend to feel sympathy with his disappointments. Oh, this sounds so cruel and heartless, maybe I am too involved in the theory underlying overt, dynamic behaviour to cope with its consequences.

CHAPTER 9

Interview with Susan

Fred and I grew rather apart in the last couple of years at school ever since Fred went to that posh St Malcolm's. He became very close to Dad and I felt pushed aside by both of them and left to my own devices. Until then I had always been Dad's favourite, at least until my elopement with Adonis. But eventually Fred and I were drawn together again.

One night Fred and I settled down in his room for a quiet conversation about the family. It seemed to both of us that Dad looked very troubled and depressed lately. We were wondering whether he was in some kind of financial trouble or perhaps had entered male menopause. After a lot of talk we decided that it could only be the latter. Fred said that compared to the fathers of his best friends, our father seemed to suffer from a very faint image. These other men were always flying jet planes, taking over companies and one was even involved in gun-running and maybe the Mafia. What we needed to do to buck him up was to find him a better image. So we started to weigh ideas. Obviously for a bank manager, the best image to build was that of a daring, financial wizard, buying and selling uranium and other interesting stuff, and playing the stock exchange, bringing home the most incredible winners. On the other hand, he must also maintain his personal popularity by free lending policies to his friends. And I suggested he should acquire a debonair manner like the Benson and Hedges man, which would attract the most glamorous women in the world.

As we filled out this picture of Dad's new ego, it occurred to us almost simultaneously that this would leave Mum behind in a most unfair position. A little old hick psychiatrist could hardly compete

Lost in the Freudian Forest

We filled out this picture of Dad's new ego

Interview with Susan

when Dad was exposed to all these glamorous women. Even now she was dull compared to my best friend's mother who had had three divorces. However, we didn't want glamorous girlfriends to lead to a messy divorce in our house so we decided firmly that we must do everything possible to preserve the sanctity of the family. The solution to this problem was quite easy: We would give Mother's image a facelift too and decided to start in the realm of her professional life. I could see a Female Freud of the Twentieth Century emerging to make our town as famous as Vienna. With women's liberation, even professional fame like that of the great Freud should be attainable for female psychiatrists. Fred suggested that perhaps she should advertise or have a TV show like David Frost or Graham Kerr. We had to discard this idea as far too ambitious for our pockets at that time. Then I showed Fred one of my treasures. A hobby of mine over the years has been reading Mother's case histories and filling a notebook with the more interesting ones. This led us to a way of resolving what to do about making Mum's career more exciting. Our local newspaper published "Notes from a Doctor's Diary" every week and we decided to send along some of Mum's best cases in the form of a column headed "The psychiatrist says...". We couldn't publish her name, but if we told all our friends the word would soon get round, and some of her patients might recognise themselves and realise they were famous and tell their friends too.

We set all this into practice immediately. Both Fred and I told our friends about our glamorous father, who was constantly on the phone to London, Paris and New York to arrange share deals or commodity transactions. We whispered that he even talks to a man in the Kremlin occasionally who has interesting tips about the uranium market. We passed on imaginary details about all-night parties at the office to celebrate his successes. We mentioned that he felt he was at last practising modern banking methods which must develop not only to be more daring, but also must incorporate a more liberal attitude to customers' financial needs. I am sure the stories got around to the parents of these kids, because the image we painted for him was quite irresistible and most of our friends must have felt that it was the sort of Dad they would like to have.

With Mother's case, things were off to a slower start. We began

74 Lost in the Freudian Forest

our column with the account by Mrs X of one of her dreams:

"Just after I had gone to bed one night my bedroom door was pushed open and a great big brown monkey climbed into my bed and cuddled up to me. It was quite pleasant and comfortable. Suddenly he jumped up and changed his shape—he turned into a huge snake. I screamed and escaped from the room and he was following me down the corridor, which became a railway track. He came closer and closer and touched me and then everything exploded. I woke up and was in my bed with my father standing next to me. He was rather anxious because I had awoken him with my screaming."

It was disappointing that Mum's only comment in her notes was to make another appointment for 2 p.m. on Thursday. We had been reading Freud ourselves since we were very young and recognised the symbolism immediately, so we supplied the following interpretation ourselves:

"Dear Mrs X,
You have obviously tried to seduce your father, who was the monkey in your dream. He turned into a snake, which represents a penis. This chased you down the corridor where you had intercourse, as symbolised by the explosion."

We were very pleased with this first effort and felt Mrs X would benefit too.

We put some quite hard work into this campaign to improve our parents' image and felt we should have some results soon. Then one evening Dad was reading the newspaper when he gave a shout of derisive laughter and pushed the paper in front of Mother, saying "Here's one of your colleagues publishing a lot of rubbishy psychoanalytic fantasy, and probably getting paid for it too". Mum took a while to read the letter and then screamed: "But this is right out of my case file—it's unethical—I'll be ruined! And this on top of all the gossip about your goings-on in the bank!" Dad was astonished. She told him about the stories of his reckless gambling on the world's stock exchanges and the champagne parties at the office. We felt this was a bad start for their new roles and things might improve if they could talk it over a bit more, but just then the telephone rang and Dad was called to the office because an inspector had turned up unexpectedly.

He turned into a huge snake

Dad was reading the newspaper when he gave a shout of derisive laughter

The upshot of all this was that Dad was suspended from the bank for three months while investigations into his dealings were going on, and Mum had a letter calling her before the ethics committee of the medical association on a complaint from Mrs X. Mum argued with Dad that we were not to be punished for our part in the drama because our intentions had been good and our motives of the highest order. I think she only won the argument when she pointed out that child beating wouldn't help his reputation at the bank. However, she did break some of her own rules and gave us a very punishing lecture about what we had done to her professional standing.

We felt disappointed that they weren't going to get much benefit from our hard work, but we weren't too worried. We knew the enquiry into Dad's affairs must be dismissed since he had a completely clean slate, and that the charge against Mother would come to nothing. We felt that we really had done very little harm, and that we had achieved some pretty good image building in spite of the minor inconveniences for our parents which resulted from the two enquiries. Privately, we were convinced that any publicity is good publicity.

EXTRACT FROM MARIGOLD GOLEM'S DIARY

April 1

I have noticed a new wave of whispering between Susan and Fred. They seem to be planning some co-operative venture. This is a welcome change of scene and I am sure it will be therapeutic for Fred after his disappointment with Trevor's value system. (Although I must admit that Fred bore his cross with dignity and maturity.) It will also be good for Susan, who may have found it rough going lately—a let down from the days of her blooming romance with young Adonis Sebastian. Maybe it was all to the good, since Adonis may have saved her from Trevor rather than Trevor from Adonis. It is all so confusing, sometimes the collective psychoanalytic mind boggles.

April 21

I have heard rumours that Fred and Susan are spreading stories everywhere about Trevor's daring financial escapades and about his wild sexual orgies at the bank offices. What a laugh—poor Trevor who is so scrupulously honest in his running of the bank and so lacking in libido where sex is concerned. However, the twins' behaviour must be recognised in the context of their own relationship to a father figure. They find Trevor at present an unsatisfactory object for identification with maleness. This is relative to filmstars like Peter Ustinov or Charles Boyer—two objects whom even I find very attractive. Therefore, in their fantasy they build up this new image of their father for more satisfactory identification. Then, not content with their own fantasy which would be similar to masturbation, they spread these stories so that they can share their creation with their friends. It could be a new, as yet unidentified defence mechanism: Reality Tested Fantasy Identification (RTFI). I must work this idea out in more detail as it develops. I am very pleased that this RTFI is confined to Trevor, it reassures me that I am a satisfactory object for identification. It is better for me not to try to explain any of this to Trevor at the moment.

May 15

This has been the worst week of my life. First Trevor showed me a newspaper column with a case history which can only have come from my file. It must be the work of the twins. Then I blurted out to Trevor about the twins telling these stories to their friends. Finally, we heard there will be a double investigation by the Bank and by the Medical Association. Nothing can save us from a public scandal.

I also have failed to provide the children with an adequate image for identification. Even if I am acquitted by the Ethics Committee, this failure is something which is difficult to live with. I feel at the end of my wits. Maybe I am a misfit and should give up psychiatry and motherhood and be content with homebuilding.

Letter from Trevor Golem to his brother Bert

May 15

Dear Bert,

I am going through a series of crises. Fred's two years at St Malcolm's have shown me that even these great private schools are a hypocritical fraud, a creation of the devil. This was followed by an investigation into my handling of the bank's financial affairs, where of course I was cleared completely. Yet I feel that after twenty-five years of faithful service, I should have been treated with more trust and consideration. Banks lack humanity and see only their profits; again I feel they use us in the service of the devil. Marigold is also in a very bad state, her charming, cheerful personality has given way to constant deep despair. I feel I should give up banking and become a good professional Christian like you, Bert. I know you will understand me.

Yours in brotherly love,

Trevor

Telegram from Bert Golem to his brother Trevor

MABEL AND I PRAY DAILY FOR THE DELIVERANCE OF YOUR POOR TORMENTED SOUL CHEERS BERT

CHAPTER 10

Interview with Fred and Susan

Fred began the account of the last few days:
After our rather disastrous efforts to improve our parents' self and public image we had a session to discuss our own future. We thought the time had come to be less altruistic and to turn more attention to ourselves. One of Mother's favourite topics was the importance of self-actualisation and self-fulfilment which, according to a guy called Maslow, were high on man's hierarchy of needs. She said it was only the rare individual who was fortunate enough to attain this state of Nirvana. Mother said the process began with a realisation of one's full potential, an achievement which also provided an investment in one's future.

Starting on the first step of this ladder, Susan, who had been very successful in the last school play, proceeded to ring up a film studio in response to an advertisement for extras and made an appointment for an audition. She set off groomed to a tee with Mother's wig, a healthy helping of Mother's make-up, a sophisticated dress and platform shoes borrowed from a girlfriend. She looked really like nobody I had ever seen before—sort of stunning—and I was sure she was irresistible with this outfit and her dramatic talents. It was a surprise when she returned crestfallen, mortified by the uncouth film executives and blaming their ignorance for her failure. She said they had roared with laughter when she walked in and sent her away without a screen test. She vowed never to try this art form again since it was so crude. She even began to doubt that the cinema could be called a form of art. Seeking another method for realisation of her undoubted potential, she started to write a novel. It was designed to be an insightful story based on her own eventful young life, filled with such tragic moments

An insightful story... her affair with Adonis

as her affair with Adonis. I thought it was beautiful and the title was derived from Mum's philosophy: "In search of self-fulfilment". I am not ashamed to admit that I had tears in my eyes when I first read it. Yet it received a cold uninformative rejection slip from every publisher whose name we could find in the telephone directory. I am sure it was far too subtle and insightful for them to understand.

In the meantime I had also been busy with my self-development. First, I wrote to a number of people overseas: I offered my services as a social secretary to a polar explorer for his next trip. Then I wrote to the US space agency and to the President of the Supreme Soviet offering my services as an astronaut for their space programmes, mentioning in both cases my training at Camp Endeavour. There were no replies at all. Then I turned my attention to the local scene. I answered an advertisement for an aide-de-camp to the Governor. I was quite sure I would succeed this time since the Governor was an old boy from St Malcolm's and would favour those who wore the same school tie. I came nearer to success this time: I got a reply signed by the Governor's secretary regretting that another applicant had been given the post. I saw in the paper the following week that he was only a university graduate who had not even been to St Malcolm's.

After all these rejections, Susan and I wandered desolate and desperate down to the new shopping centre in search of consolation. We found this in a milk bar over a chocolate sundae and somewhat recovered, we repaired to the supermarket to admire the consumer society at its most aggressive. We were accosted by a young man attired as a clown, who handed us a leaflet. It promised selected entrants an opportunity in a quiz show with first prize of a seventeen-day luxury cruise to the Bahamas. To enter the competition one had to write a slogan to advertise a new toilet paper made by my friend's father, Torpington-Smith. Susan's literary talent provided her with inspiration immediately. We carefully wrote: "Torpington's Toilet Tissues—Better for Baby's Bottom" on the form and dropped it into the box provided for this purpose.

A week later we received a letter inviting us to the quiz show. We spent the next few days memorising all the rivers in Asia and the Guiness Book of Records. We arrived at the TV station well prepared with dictionaries, encyclopaedia and other reference works which we were asked to leave in the cloakroom. I was trembling when we stood before the camera and the quiz master asked us three questions each. They all concerned Torpington's toilet tissue or related products. We said we used it by the yard and how good it was, and oh how soft. We knew it came in three colours, and two fresh-air scents, and was approved by the Department of Health and Environment, and so on. It was all dead easy and we won. We were hugged and congratulated and signed a contract promising to advertise "Twin tissue packs" and finally we were handed two envelopes with tickets and spending money. We rushed home to celebrate but Mum was at a psychiatric centre for neglected teenagers, and Dad was locked in his study working on a statement for the bank's auditors which he had been trying unsuccessfully to write for weeks. We spent the evening excitedly packing suitcases for our departure on the cruise ship next day. At breakfast Mum didn't appear and Dad was too moody to talk to, so we put a note on the kitchen table and left.

Susan took up the story at this stage:

Fred and I really enjoyed the trip. It was an entirely new world for us, one we had never lived in before. We drifted into the daily routine of the cruise without effort—deck games, swimming and lying in the sunshine all day; and in the evening, dances, fancy dress parties, "horse racing" and other games. We didn't have to worry about anything—the cruise director was always at hand to help. When there were shore excursions, they were planned for us and all arrangements were made by the purser. We immediately became part of the crowd and did everything with the same group of people.

Life was very busy, but occasionally we would think about home life and wonder about Mother's philosophy. She had always emphasised self-sufficiency and to this end had worried about the resolution of our various complexes. She preached that we would derive satisfaction (and self-actualisation) from accepting responsibility for ourselves and others. Yet here we were, with no call to be self-sufficient nor responsible and having a thoroughly good time.

She taught us to abhor rules and structure, but we found the shipboard day-to-day routine and organisation made life very easy. It dawned on us that the "free" environment that Mum had been so careful to create was in fact highly structured by her expectations. What made her world more difficult to live in than our present one was that she imposed structure without any guide to action.

Mum was honestly convinced that her method was the only true path to happiness. Now we found that not only were there other paths, there were also other happinesses. We wondered if Mother would be surprised that our present delightful life was not due to self-actualisation, nor to the resolution of complexes, nor to superior insight; it had required no more skill than winning at roulette.

We wrote a long letter to Mum suggesting she review her theory. We explained that order can be enjoyable, that rules need not be restrictive and that paternalistic adults can be a comforting presence (even at the age of eighteen!)

The only answer from home was the following letter from Dad:

Dear Twins,
You have been gone for only one week and we miss you very much. Your letter to Mother arrived but she didn't give it to me to read. Your mother is not her usual self. She sits most of the time and just stares into her tea cup, muttering to herself that Freud has failed her. She sometimes starts to talk and then stops without finishing a sentence. She also neglects her appearance and you know how fussy she used to be over her hair and polished nails. Only very rarely does she go to her consulting rooms. There were some signs of this over the past few weeks, although you may not have noticed it, but since your sudden departure with only a farewell note, she has become so much worse. I think she feels she has failed as a mother, wife and psychiatrist and that everything has gone wrong, that her good intentions have misfired. But these are our worries and you shouldn't let them interfere with your trip. I hope you have a good time and that things will be more cheerful at home when you return.

Love,

Dad.

It was sad that Mum felt so bad about having brought us up according to the book of Freud and that we had turned out different to her expectations. We didn't worry about it for too long and went back to playing table tennis.

Two days later the cruise ended and Dad met us at the wharf with a very worried face and told us that Mum had had a breakdown and that he had asked you as her oldest friends to come at once.

EXTRACT FROM MARIGOLD GOLEM'S DIARY

July 14

A letter from the twins today... My god, what have I created... they are no different to ordinary people! What I think of my aims for them—to be unique individuals, resourceful, independent of others. Now they're penned up on a cruise ship, enjoying mass entertainment with the rest of the sheep, Baaaa! And they have the nerve to accuse me of having overstructured their early life. After all the papers I have written about child rearing! I should have had an abortion! What went wrong? It can't have been my fault. Could it be the theory? But Freud couldn't be wrong! Could he? Could Freud make a mistake? Should I change the theory? No! Easier to change the twins. God, what a mess. I wish I'd never heard of Freud. Don't trust Freud... Don't trust Freud... Don't trust Freud.

Psychiatrists' Report

Now that we have collected the case material on the Golem family we have come to the following conclusions.

The problem, we feel, arose out of Marigold's fanatical adherence to her theory and her expectations that the children would provide a unique model for a new generation. She thought she could create paragons of the virtue which she valued most: unlimited self-actualisation. The children, in Marigold's eyes, were disappointingly normal. Her diary shows that for a long time she misinterpreted their behaviour to fit her own views. When the discrepancy between reality and expectations finally became apparent, she became profoundly depressed.

Being psychiatrists we cannot resist the temptation to describe yet another theoretical concept, to be known in the future as the "Pygmalion Syndrome". It is the desire to create a person according to a detailed, idealised image. Marigold was suffering from this syndrome when she attempted to create the twins according to an image arising from her theory. Trevor to a lesser extent tried to create an image from his own ambitions and fantasies when he sent Fred to St Malcolm's. Parents the whole world over attempt to make their children into something that they are not meant to be. Fantasy, frustrated ambition and striving for better life styles form the basis for this "Pygmalion Syndrome".

We ourselves feel one problem was that Marigold's theory, like so many others, was a misinterpretation of Freudian psychoanalytic practices. But the main fault lay in adopting a prescription as being the one and only way to bring up a child.

It is interesting that Trevor, typically conservative and inflexible, could survive his disappointments with the children better than Marigold who saw herself as far more emotionally robust. The fact that the twins turned into "normal" young adults demonstrates the fortunate resilience of children in surviving the mistakes of their parents.